MASSACHUSETTS TEST PREP

PARCC Practice Book

Mathematics

Grade 5

ISBN 978-1502486981

CONTENTS

INTRODUCTION
For Parents, Teachers, and Tutors

About the PARCC Assessments

Students in Massachusetts may be assessed each year by taking a set of tests known as the PARCC assessments. The two main assessments are the Performance-Based Assessment (PBA) and the End-of-Year Assessment (EOY). This book has two complete PBA practice tests and two complete EOY practice tests. The practice tests have the same format, the same question types, and cover the same skills as the real assessments. Further information on the PBA and the EOY is included in the introduction to each practice test.

Key Features of the PARCC Assessments

The PARCC assessments have key features that students will need to be familiar with, including new question styles and formats. These key features are described below.

- The tests are based on the Common Core State Standards and are strongly focused on showing an in-depth understanding of the skills described in the standards.
- The tests include a wider range of question types. There are more constructed response questions, more rigorous selected response questions, more questions involving advanced tasks, and more questions that involve providing explanations or justifying answers.
- The tests are taken online and include computer-based questions. These involve tasks like ordering numbers, selecting points on a number line or graph, sorting items, completing number sentences and equations, and using fraction models.
- The tests include more multi-step problems, more questions that involve applying skills in real-world contexts, and questions that involve complex procedures.

This book has been specifically designed to prepare students for these key features. The questions have a wide range of formats, including questions that mimic the computer-based formats. The questions are more rigorous and include more advanced tasks. The skills assessed match the PARCC tests, with a greater focus on applying skills and on demonstrating in-depth understanding.

About the Common Core State Standards

The *Massachusetts Curriculum Frameworks* describe the skills that students are expected to have. These frameworks are based on the Common Core State Standards. They incorporate all the Common Core standards, as well as some additional skills. Just like the real PARCC assessments, the questions in this book test whether students have the knowledge and skills described in the Common Core State Standards.

INTRODUCTION TO THE PBA PRACTICE TEST
For Parents, Teachers, and Tutors

About the Performance-Based Assessment

The Performance-Based Assessment (PBA) is taken after about 75% of the school year is complete. The PBA focuses on applying skills and concepts to solve problems. The emphasis is on completing multi-step problems and advanced tasks. This test is made up of three different types of items, as described below.

- **Type I** – these items are straightforward selected response or simple computer-based questions. These items are worth 1 or 2 points.

- **Type II** – these items are constructed response questions that involve completing more complex tasks and usually require students to show their work, explain their answer, or provide justifications. These items are worth 3 or 4 points.

- **Type III** – these items are complex constructed response questions that involve modeling or applying skills in real-world contexts. These items are worth 3 or 6 points.

The actual test contains 9 Type I items, 4 Type II items, and 3 Type III items. The practice tests in this book contains more questions of each type, especially more Type II and Type III items. This will ensure that students experience all the types of questions they are likely to encounter on the real test and gain the experience needed to complete more rigorous tasks.

Taking the Test

Just like the real EOY test, the practice test is divided into two sessions. Each session includes 15 questions. On the real test, students are allowed 2 hours to complete each session. To account for the additional questions, students should be allowed 4 hours for each session of the practice test. Students can complete the two sessions on the same day or on different days, but should have a break between sessions.

Calculators and Tools

Students should be provided with a ruler and a protractor to use on both sessions of the test. Students are not allowed to use a calculator on any session of the PARCC tests, and so should complete all the practice tests without the use of a calculator. Students may also use the information on the Reference Sheet included on the first page of the test.

PARCC Performance-Based Assessment

Practice Test 1

Session 1

Instructions

Read each question carefully. For each multiple-choice question, fill in the circle for the correct answer. For other types of questions, follow the directions given in the question.

Some questions may ask you to show your work. Be sure to show your work or explain how you found your answer in the space provided.

You may use a ruler and a protractor to help you answer questions. You may not use a calculator on this test. You may use the information below to help you answer questions.

REFERENCE INFORMATION

1 mile = 5,280 feet	1 pound = 16 ounces	1 cup = 8 fluid ounces
1 mile = 1,760 yards	1 ton = 2,000 pounds	1 pint = 2 cups
		1 quart = 2 pints
		1 gallon = 4 quarts
		1 liter = 1000 cubic centimeters

Right Rectangular Prism $V = Bh$ or $V = lwh$

1   The table below shows the ticket prices for a bus tour.

Ticket	Price
Adult	$5
Child	$3
Senior	$4

Sam's family paid exactly $15 for bus tickets. Which set of tickets could they have bought?

Ⓐ   1 adult, 2 child, and 1 senior

Ⓑ   2 adult, 1 child

Ⓒ   1 adult, 1 child, 2 senior

Ⓓ   3 child, 1 senior

2   Amanda plotted the four points below on a coordinate grid.

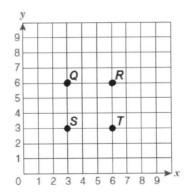

Amanda plots a fifth point that is an equal distance from two of the points. Which of these could be the coordinates of the fifth point?

Ⓐ   (5, 8)

Ⓑ   (3.5, 5)

Ⓒ   (7, 7)

Ⓓ   (9, 4.5)

3   A bakery sold 0.25 of its apple pies by lunch time. What fraction of the apple pies were sold by lunch time?

Ⓐ $\dfrac{1}{25}$

Ⓑ $\dfrac{1}{4}$

Ⓒ $\dfrac{2}{5}$

Ⓓ $\dfrac{3}{4}$

4   Place the shapes below in order from the least sides to the most sides.

octagon   triangle   hexagon   square   pentagon

Least   _____

_____

_____

_____

Most   _____

5   Jed has 12 dimes, 18 nickels, and 42 pennies. What is the greatest common factor Jed can use to divide the coins into equal piles? Circle the correct answer.

  2   3   4   6   8   12

6   Erin is sorting 65 quarters into piles. She puts the quarters in piles of 5.

Complete the number sentence below to show how many piles of quarters Erin has.

_____ ÷ _____ = _____

7   Joanne had three singing lessons one week. Two lessons went for 45 minutes, and one lesson went for 60 minutes. Which number sentence could be used to find how many minutes Joanne had singing lessons for?

Ⓐ   (2 x 45) x 60

Ⓑ   (2 + 45) x 60

Ⓒ   (2 x 45) + 60

Ⓓ   (2 + 45) + 60

8   A school has 7 school buses. Each bus can seat 48 students. A total of 303 students get on the buses to go to a school camp. How many empty seats would there be on the buses?

Show your work.

Answer _____

9   What is the value of the expression below?

$$(16 + 20) - 8 \div 4$$

Show your work.

Answer _____

10   A jug of milk contains 3 quarts of milk. Michael pours 1 pint of milk from the jug. How many pints of milk are left in the jug?

Show your work.

Answer _____ pints

11   A talent contest will go for 100 minutes. The contest is divided into 16 equal segments. How long will each segment go for? You can use the hundreds grid below to help you find your answer.

Show your work.

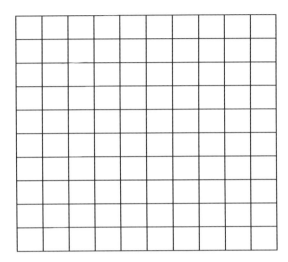

Answer _____ minutes

12   Mike went on vacation to Ohio. When he left home, the odometer read 7,219.4 miles. When he returned home, the odometer read 8,192.6 miles. How many miles did Mike travel?

Show your work.

Answer _____ miles

13   The table below shows the prices of items at a cake stall.

Item	Price
Small cake	$1.85
Muffin	$2.25
Cookie	$0.95

Frankie bought a small cake and a cookie. Bronwyn bought a muffin. How much more did Frankie spend than Bronwyn?

Show your work.

Answer _____

14   The grid below represents Dani's living room.

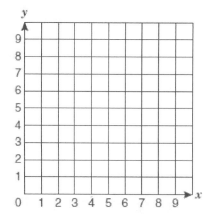

The television is located at the point (5, 4). A lamp is sitting 4 units to the right of the television and 3 units down from the television. What ordered pair represents the location of the lamp?

Answer _____

Explain how you found your answer.

_____

_____

_____

_____

_____

15   Justine drew the triangle XYZ below.

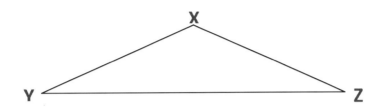

Based on the side lengths, what type of triangle is XYZ?

Answer _____

Explain why you classified the triangle that way.

_____

_____

_____

_____

_____

END OF SESSION 1

PARCC Performance-Based Assessment

Practice Test 1

Session 2

Instructions

Read each question carefully. For each multiple-choice question, fill in the circle for the correct answer. For other types of questions, follow the directions given in the question.

Some questions may ask you to show your work. Be sure to show your work or explain how you found your answer in the space provided.

You may use a ruler and a protractor to help you answer questions. You may not use a calculator on this test. You may use the information below to help you answer questions.

REFERENCE INFORMATION

1 mile = 5,280 feet	1 pound = 16 ounces	1 cup = 8 fluid ounces
1 mile = 1,760 yards	1 ton = 2,000 pounds	1 pint = 2 cups
		1 quart = 2 pints
		1 gallon = 4 quarts
		1 liter = 1000 cubic centimeters

Right Rectangular Prism $V = Bh$ or $V = lwh$

16 · The table below shows the total cost of hiring DVDs for different numbers of DVDs.

Number of DVDs (d)	Total Cost, in Dollars (C)
2	6
5	15
6	18
8	24

Write an equation that describes the relationship between the number of DVDs hired, d, and the total cost in dollars, C. Write your equation below.

_____

17 Which of the following shapes is a pentagon?

Ⓐ

Ⓑ

Ⓒ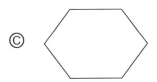

Ⓓ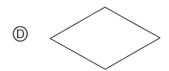

18 At the start of the week, a plant had a height of $\frac{5}{8}$ inches. The plant grew $\frac{1}{4}$ of an inch during the week. Which diagram is shaded to show the height of the plant at the end of the week?

Ⓐ

Ⓑ

Ⓒ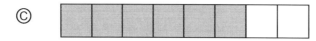

Ⓓ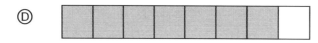

19 On May 1, Felipe paid $3.58 per gallon of fuel. On August 1, Felipe paid $3.71 per gallon of fuel. By how much did the price of fuel increase?

Ⓐ $0.03

Ⓑ $0.07

Ⓒ $0.13

Ⓓ $0.17

20 Which operation in the expression should be carried out first?

$$6 + 3 \times (8 - 2 \times 2)$$

Ⓐ $6 + 3$

Ⓑ 3×8

Ⓒ $8 - 2$

Ⓓ 2×2

21 Bryant was reading a book with 220 pages. He read 90 pages in the first week. He wants to finish the book in 5 days. Which expression can be used to calculate how many pages he needs to read each day to finish the book in 5 days?

Ⓐ $220 \div 5 - 90$

Ⓑ $220 - 90 \div 5$

Ⓒ $220 - (90 \div 5)$

Ⓓ $(220 - 90) \div 5$

22 The width of a football field is 160 feet. What is the width of the football field in yards? Write your answer below.

_____ yards

23 Harris and Jamie both started with no savings. Harris saved $3 per week, while Jamie saved $6 per week.

Part A

Complete the table below to show Harris's and Jamie's total savings at the end of each week for the first 6 weeks.

Week	1	2	3	4	5	6
Harris's Total Savings						
Jamie's Total Savings						

Part B

Describe the relationship between Harris's total savings and Jamie's total savings each week.

_____

_____

_____

_____

_____

24 The list below shows data a science class collected on the diameter of hailstones that fell during a storm.

Hailstone Diameter (inches)

$$\frac{1}{4}, \frac{1}{4}, \frac{1}{2}, \frac{5}{8}, \frac{1}{2}, \frac{3}{8}, \frac{5}{8}, \frac{1}{4}, \frac{7}{8}, \frac{3}{4}$$

Part A

Plot the data on the line plot below.

Hailstone Diameter (inches)

0	$\frac{1}{8}$	$\frac{1}{4}$	$\frac{3}{8}$	$\frac{1}{2}$	$\frac{5}{8}$	$\frac{3}{4}$	$\frac{7}{8}$	1

Part B

The median is the middle value when the diameters are placed in order. Use the line plot you made to find the median diameter.

Answer _____ inch

Explain how you used the line plot to find your answer.

_____

_____

_____

_____

25   Tom worked for 32 hours and earned $448. He earned the same rate per hour.

Part A

Write an equation that can be solved to find how much Tom earns per hour. Use *h* to represent how much Tom earns per hour.

Equation _____

Part B

Solve the equation to find much Tom earns per hour.

Show your work.

Answer _____

26   Mitch ran 2.6 miles on Monday and 1.8 miles on Tuesday. How many miles less did Mitch run on Tuesday? Use the diagram below to find the answer.

Answer _____ miles

Explain how you used the diagram to find your answer.

_____

_____

_____

_____

27 The model below is made up of 1-centimeter cubes. What is the volume of the model?

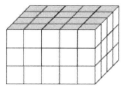

Show your work.

Answer _____ cubic centimeters

28   Joe made the graph below to show the locations of prizes he hid for a treasure hunt. Each star represents a treasure.

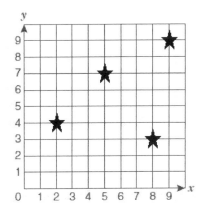

Which ordered pair represents the treasure located closest to the origin?

Show your work.

Answer _____

29   Sushi sells for $3 for each small roll and $5 for each large roll.

Derrick bought 4 small rolls and 7 large rolls.

Part A

Complete the expression below to show how to find the total amount Derrick spent, in dollars.

$$(\underline{\quad} \times \underline{\quad}) + (\underline{\quad} \times \underline{\quad})$$

Part B

Simplify the expression you wrote to find the total amount Derrick spent.

Show your work.

Answer $_____

30   There are 200 students at Kerry's elementary school. Of those students, $\frac{2}{5}$ are fifth grade students. How many fifth grade students are there?

Show your work.

Answer _____

END OF SESSION 2

INTRODUCTION TO THE EOY PRACTICE TEST
For Parents, Teachers, and Tutors

About the End-of-Year Assessment

The End-of-Year Assessment (EOY) is taken after about 90% of the school year is complete. It is designed to allow students to demonstrate that they have the skills and knowledge described in the Common Core State Standards. The EOY Assessment only includes the Type I questions described below.

- **Type I** – these items are straightforward selected response or simple computer-based questions. These items are worth 1 or 2 points.

These items may be simple selected response questions where the one correct answer is selected or selected response questions with 2 or more correct answers. The computer-based questions could involve writing numerical answers, sorting or ordering numbers or items, selecting points on a number line or graph, completing number sentences and equations, or using fraction models. This practice test includes a wide range of formats that mimic the computer-based questions.

The actual test contains 36 Type I items. The practice tests in this book contain 50 Type I items. This will ensure that students have practice with all the types of questions they are likely to encounter on the real test and gain the experience needed to complete questions with a range of new formats.

Taking the Test

Just like the real EOY test, the practice test is divided into two sessions. Each session includes 25 questions. On the real test, students are allowed 2 hours to complete each session. To account for the additional questions, students should be allowed 3 hours for each session of the practice test. Students can complete the two sessions on the same day or on different days, but should have a break between sessions.

Calculators and Tools

Students should be provided with a ruler and a protractor to use on both sessions of the test. Students are not allowed to use a calculator on any session of the PARCC tests, and so should complete all the practice tests without the use of a calculator. Students may also use the information on the Reference Sheet included on the first page of the test.

PARCC End-of-Year Assessment

Practice Test 1

Session 1

Instructions

Read each question carefully. For each multiple-choice question, fill in the circle for the correct answer. For other types of questions, follow the directions given in the question.

You may use a ruler and a protractor to help you answer questions. You may not use a calculator on this test. You may use the information below to help you answer questions.

REFERENCE INFORMATION

1 mile = 5,280 feet	1 pound = 16 ounces	1 cup = 8 fluid ounces
1 mile = 1,760 yards	1 ton = 2,000 pounds	1 pint = 2 cups
		1 quart = 2 pints
		1 gallon = 4 quarts
		1 liter = 1000 cubic centimeters

Right Rectangular Prism $V = Bh$ or $V = lwh$

1 To add the fractions below, Wayne first needs to determine the least common multiple of the denominators.

$$\frac{1}{5}, \frac{5}{7}, \frac{9}{10}$$

What is the least common multiple of the denominators? Write your answer below.

_____

2 The diagram below shows the length of a piece of ribbon.

$$\frac{12}{100} \text{ meter}$$

Victoria divides the lace into 4 equal pieces. What is the length of each piece of lace?

Ⓐ $\frac{2}{25}$ meter

Ⓑ $\frac{3}{25}$ meter

Ⓒ $\frac{12}{25}$ meter

Ⓓ $\frac{3}{100}$ meter

3   Donna has $8.45. She spends $3.75. How much money does Donna have left? Write your answer below.

$_____

4   Hannah cut out a piece of fabric to use for an art project. The length of the fabric was 9.5 yards. The width of the fabric was 3.6 yards less than the length. What was the width of the fabric?

    Ⓐ   5.9 yards

    Ⓑ   6.9 yards

    Ⓒ   12.1 yards

    Ⓓ   13.1 yards

5   Errol is putting photos into albums. Each album has 24 pages for holding photos, and each page can hold 8 photographs. How many photographs could Errol put into 3 photo albums?

    Ⓐ   192

    Ⓑ   376

    Ⓒ   486

    Ⓓ   576

6   Kathy answered $\frac{3}{5}$ of the questions on a test correctly. Which of the following is equivalent to $\frac{3}{5}$?

Ⓐ   0.3

Ⓑ   0.35

Ⓒ   0.6

Ⓓ   0.65

7   Which ordered pairs represent a point where the edges of the two rectangles intersect? Select **all** the correct answers.

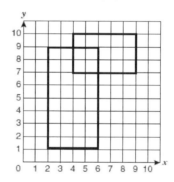

☐   (8, 6)

☐   (6, 7)

☐   (5, 8)

☐   (4, 10)

☐   (7, 9)

☐   (4, 9)

8   To complete a calculation correctly, Mark moves the decimal place of 420.598 two places to the left.

$$420.598 \rightarrow 4.20598$$

Which of these describes the calculation completed?

Ⓐ   Dividing by 10

Ⓑ   Dividing by 100

Ⓒ   Multiplying by 10

Ⓓ   Multiplying by 100

9   Camille cooked a cake on high for $1\frac{1}{4}$ hours. She then cooked it for another $\frac{1}{2}$ hour on low. How long did she cook the cake for in all?

Ⓐ $1\frac{1}{2}$ hours

Ⓑ $1\frac{3}{4}$ hours

Ⓒ $2\frac{1}{4}$ hours

Ⓓ $2\frac{1}{2}$ hours

10   A play sold $224 worth of tickets. Each ticket cost the same amount. Which of these could be the cost of each ticket? Select **all** the possible answers.

☐ $6

☐ $8

☐ $12

☐ $14

☐ $16

☐ $18

11   A piece of note paper has side lengths of 12.5 centimeters. What is the area of the piece of note paper?

Ⓐ   144.25 square centimeters

Ⓑ   144.5 square centimeters

Ⓒ   156.25 square centimeters

Ⓓ   156.5 square centimeters

12   Cody drew a quadrilateral on a coordinate grid, as shown below.

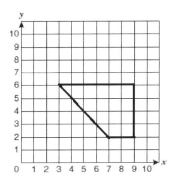

What are the coordinates of the vertices of the quadrilateral? Write the coordinates below.

(___, ___)   (___, ___)   (___, ___)   (___, ___)

13   Sandy has $12.90. Marvin has $18.50. What is the total value of their money? Write your answer below.

$ _____

14   The top of a desk is 4 feet long and 3 feet wide. Raymond wants to cover the top of the desk with a vinyl sheet. The vinyl sheet is measured in square inches. What is the area of the vinyl sheet that will cover the top of the desk exactly?

   Ⓐ   12 square inches

   Ⓑ   144 square inches

   Ⓒ   168 square inches

   Ⓓ   1,728 square inches

15 A block is in the shape of a cube. If the side length is represented by *x*, which of these could be used to find the volume of the cube?

Ⓐ $3x$

Ⓑ $6(x^2)$

Ⓒ $6x$

Ⓓ x^3

16 Denise made the line plot below to show how long she read for each weekday for 4 weeks.

Daily Reading Time (hours)

	X			
X			X	
X		X	X	
X		X	X	X
X	X	X	X	X
X	X	X	X	X
0	$\frac{1}{4}$	$\frac{1}{2}$	$\frac{3}{4}$	1

How long did Denise read for in total over the 4 weeks? Write your answer below.

_____ hours

17 The point below is translated 2 units to the left and 3 units down. What are the coordinates of the point after the translation?

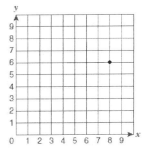

Ⓐ   (6, 3)

Ⓑ   (6, 9)

Ⓒ   (10, 3)

Ⓓ   (10, 9)

18 The table below shows the total number of pounds of flour in different numbers of bags of flour.

Number of Bags	Number of Pounds
3	12
5	20
8	32
9	36

Based on the relationship in the table, how much flour is in each bag? Give your answer in pounds and then ounces. Write your answers below.

_____ pounds

_____ ounces

19 The model below is made up of 1-centimeter cubes. Complete the number sentence below to find the volume of the model.

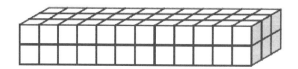

$$\boxed{} \times \boxed{} \times \boxed{} = \boxed{} \text{ cm}^3$$

20 Which decimal is plotted on the number line below?

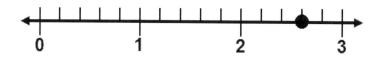

Ⓐ   2.25

Ⓑ   2.3

Ⓒ   2.6

Ⓓ   2.75

21 Brian made 16 paper cranes in 15 minutes. If he continues making cranes at this rate, how many cranes would he make in 2 hours? Write your answer below.

_____ paper cranes

22   The wingspan of the butterfly is 6.7 centimeters.

What is the wingspan of the butterfly in millimeters?

Ⓐ   0.067 mm

Ⓑ   0.67 mm

Ⓒ   67 mm

Ⓓ   670 mm

23   Jason used cubes to make the model shown below. What is the volume of the model?

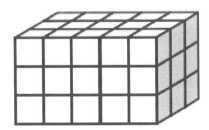

Ⓐ   15 cubic units

Ⓑ   45 cubic units

Ⓒ   50 cubic units

Ⓓ   75 cubic units

24   The pattern below starts at 0 and uses the rule "Add 4."

0, 4, 8, 12, 16

A second pattern starts at 2 and uses the rule "Add 4." How does the fifth term in the second pattern compare to the fifth term in the first pattern?

Ⓐ   It is 2 greater.

Ⓑ   It is 4 greater.

Ⓒ   It is 8 greater.

Ⓓ   It is 10 greater.

25   The table below shows a set of number pairs.

x	y
2	-2
3	0
4	2

If the points were plotted on a coordinate grid, which of the following would be the coordinates of one of the points?

Ⓐ   (0, 2)

Ⓑ   (2, 2)

Ⓒ   (4, 2)

Ⓓ   (3, 4)

END OF SESSION 1

PARCC End-of-Year Assessment

Practice Test 1

Session 2

Instructions

Read each question carefully. For each multiple-choice question, fill in the circle for the correct answer. For other types of questions, follow the directions given in the question.

You may use a ruler and a protractor to help you answer questions. You may not use a calculator on this test. You may use the information below to help you answer questions.

REFERENCE INFORMATION

1 mile = 5,280 feet
1 mile = 1,760 yards

1 pound = 16 ounces
1 ton = 2,000 pounds

1 cup = 8 fluid ounces
1 pint = 2 cups
1 quart = 2 pints
1 gallon = 4 quarts
1 liter = 1000 cubic centimeters

Right Rectangular Prism $V = Bh$ or $V = lwh$

26   The model below is made up of 1-centimeter cubes. Select the **two** correct ways to find the volume of the cube, in cubic centimeters.

☐   3 + 3 + 3

☐ 3^2

☐ 3^3

☐ $6(3^2)$

☐   9 × 6

☐   3 × 3

☐   3 × 3 × 3

27   Jason is buying baseball cards. Each packet of baseball cards contains 12 baseball cards and costs $3. How many baseball cards can Jason buy for $15? Write your answer below.

_____ baseball cards

28   Which point represents the location of the ordered pair $(1\frac{1}{4}, 2\frac{1}{2})$?

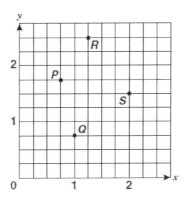

ⓐ   Point *P*

ⓑ   Point *Q*

ⓒ   Point *R*

ⓓ   Point *S*

29   Which terms describes all the shapes shown below? Select **all** the correct answers.

☐   Parallelogram

☐   Rectangle

☐   Rhombus

☐   Quadrilateral

☐   Square

30   The table below shows the total cost of hiring DVDs for different numbers of DVDs.

Number of DVDs	Total Cost, in Dollars
2	6
5	15
6	18
8	24

Which equation could be used to find the total cost in dollars, c, of hiring x DVDs?

Ⓐ $c = x + 4$

Ⓑ $c = 3x$

Ⓒ $c = x + 3$

Ⓓ $c = 8x$

31   Dave bought 4 packets of pies. Three packets had 12 pies each, and one packet had 10 pies. Which number sentence shows the total number of pies Dave bought?

Ⓐ   (3 x 12) x 10

Ⓑ   (3 + 12) x 10

Ⓒ   (3 x 12) + 10

Ⓓ   (3 + 12) + 10

32   Circle each measurement that is the same as 3 yards.

6 feet   9 feet   12 feet   18 feet

36 inches   48 inches   108 inches   144 inches

33   The table below shows the cost of hiring items from a hire store.

Item	Cost per Week
CD	$2
DVD	$3
Video game	$4

Which expression represents the total cost, in dollars, of hiring *c* CDs and *d* DVDs for *w* weeks?

Ⓐ $2c + 3d + w$

Ⓑ $w(2c + 3d)$

Ⓒ $w(2c) + 3d$

Ⓓ $2c + 3d$

34 If the numbers below were each rounded to the nearest tenth, which **two** numbers would be rounded down? Select the **two** correct answers.

☐   17.386

☐   23.758

☐   35.682

☐   54.107

☐   63.453

☐   76.935

35 The model below was made with 1-unit cubes.

What is the volume of the model? Write your answer below.

_____ cubic units

36   The graph below shows a line segment with three points marked.

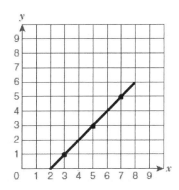

Complete the table below to show the coordinates of the three points.

x			
y			

37   Joanne had three singing lessons one week. Two lessons went for 45 minutes, and one lesson went for 60 minutes. Which number sentence could be used to find how many minutes Joanne had singing lessons for?

Ⓐ   2 x (45 + 60)

Ⓑ   (45 + 60) ÷ 3

Ⓒ   (2 x 45) + 60

Ⓓ   (2 × 45) + (2 × 60)

38   How is the numeral 9.007 written in words?

    Ⓐ   Nine and seven tenths

    Ⓑ   Nine and seven thousandths

    Ⓒ   Nine and seven hundredths

    Ⓓ   Nine thousand and seven

39   The model below shows $1\frac{6}{100}$ shaded.

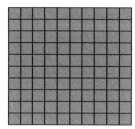 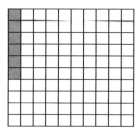

What decimal represents the shaded part of the model? Write your answer below.

_____

40   A rectangular toy box has a length of 90 centimeters, a width of 30 centimeters, and a height of 50 centimeters. What is the volume of the toy box?

    Ⓐ   4,500 cubic centimeters

    Ⓑ   6,000 cubic centimeters

    Ⓒ   81,000 cubic centimeters

    Ⓓ   135,000 cubic centimeters

41 A glass of water had a temperature of 25°C. Derek heated the water so that the temperature increased by 3°C every 10 minutes. What would the temperature of the water have been after 30 minutes?

Ⓐ   28°C

Ⓑ   31°C

Ⓒ   34°C

Ⓓ   37°C

42 Mr. Singh bought 2 adult zoo tickets for a total of $22, as well as 4 children's tickets. He spent $54 in total. How much was each children's ticket? Write your answer below.

$ _____

43 Emily cooked a roast on high for $1\frac{1}{2}$ hours. She then cooked it for another $1\frac{3}{4}$ hour on low. How long did she cook the roast for in all?

Ⓐ $2\frac{1}{4}$ hours

Ⓑ $2\frac{3}{4}$ hours

Ⓒ $3\frac{1}{4}$ hours

Ⓓ $3\frac{3}{4}$ hours

44 Which operation in the expression should be carried out first?

$$42 + 24 \div (3 - 1) + 5$$

Ⓐ   42 + 24

Ⓑ   24 ÷ 3

Ⓒ   3 − 1

Ⓓ   3 + 5

45 Leanne added $\frac{1}{4}$ cup of milk and $\frac{3}{8}$ cup of water to a bowl. Shade the diagram below to show how many cups of milk and water were in the bowl in all.

46 A bulldog weighs 768 ounces. How many pounds does the bulldog weigh?

Ⓐ   48 pounds

Ⓑ   64 pounds

Ⓒ   96 pounds

Ⓓ   192 pounds

47 The cost of renting a trailer is a basic fee of $20 plus an additional $25 for each day that the trailer is rented.

Which equation can be used to find c, the cost in dollars of the rental for d days?

Ⓐ $c = 20d + 25$

Ⓑ $c = 25d + 20$

Ⓒ $c = 20(d + 25)$

Ⓓ $c = 25(d + 20)$

48 Maxwell bought a packet of 48 baseball cards. He gave 8 baseball cards to each of 4 friends. Which number sentence can be used to find the number of baseball cards Maxwell has left?

Ⓐ $(48 - 8) \times 4$

Ⓑ $(48 - 8) \div 4$

Ⓒ $48 - (8 + 4)$

Ⓓ $48 - (8 \times 4)$

49 A square garden has side lengths of $4\frac{1}{2}$ feet. What is the area of the garden? You can use the diagram below to help find the answer.

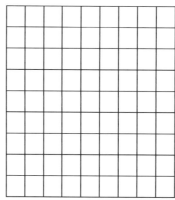

Each square is $\frac{1}{2}$ foot × $\frac{1}{2}$ foot.

Each square has an area of $\frac{1}{4}$ square feet.

Ⓐ $16\frac{1}{4}$ square feet

Ⓑ $20\frac{1}{4}$ square feet

Ⓒ $40\frac{1}{2}$ square feet

Ⓓ $182\frac{1}{4}$ square feet

50 Which two shapes have the same number of sides?

Ⓐ   Triangle and rectangle

Ⓑ   Rectangle and square

Ⓒ   Hexagon and pentagon

Ⓓ   Pentagon and triangle

END OF SESSION 2

INTRODUCTION TO THE PBA PRACTICE TEST
For Parents, Teachers, and Tutors

About the Performance-Based Assessment

The Performance-Based Assessment (PBA) is taken after about 75% of the school year is complete. The PBA focuses on applying skills and concepts to solve problems. The emphasis is on completing multi-step problems and advanced tasks. This test is made up of three different types of items, as described below.

- **Type I** – these items are straightforward selected response or simple computer-based questions. These items are worth 1 or 2 points.

- **Type II** – these items are constructed response questions that involve completing more complex tasks and usually require students to show their work, explain their answer, or provide justifications. These items are worth 3 or 4 points.

- **Type III** – these items are complex constructed response questions that involve modeling or applying skills in real-world contexts. These items are worth 3 or 6 points.

The actual test contains 9 Type I items, 4 Type II items, and 3 Type III items. The practice tests in this book contains more questions of each type, especially more Type II and Type III items. This will ensure that students experience all the types of questions they are likely to encounter on the real test and gain the experience needed to complete more rigorous tasks.

Taking the Test

Just like the real EOY test, the practice test is divided into two sessions. Each session includes 15 questions. On the real test, students are allowed 2 hours to complete each session. To account for the additional questions, students should be allowed 4 hours for each session of the practice test. Students can complete the two sessions on the same day or on different days, but should have a break between sessions.

Calculators and Tools

Students should be provided with a ruler and a protractor to use on both sessions of the test. Students are not allowed to use a calculator on any session of the PARCC tests, and so should complete all the practice tests without the use of a calculator. Students may also use the information on the Reference Sheet included on the first page of the test.

PARCC Performance-Based Assessment

Practice Test 2

Session 1

Instructions

Read each question carefully. For each multiple-choice question, fill in the circle for the correct answer. For other types of questions, follow the directions given in the question.

Some questions may ask you to show your work. Be sure to show your work or explain how you found your answer in the space provided.

You may use a ruler and a protractor to help you answer questions. You may not use a calculator on this test. You may use the information below to help you answer questions.

REFERENCE INFORMATION

1 mile = 5,280 feet
1 mile = 1,760 yards

1 pound = 16 ounces
1 ton = 2,000 pounds

1 cup = 8 fluid ounces
1 pint = 2 cups
1 quart = 2 pints
1 gallon = 4 quarts
1 liter = 1000 cubic centimeters

Right Rectangular Prism $V = Bh$ or $V = lwh$

1 Shade the diagrams below to show the subtraction. Then write the correct answer below on the blank line.

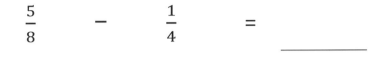

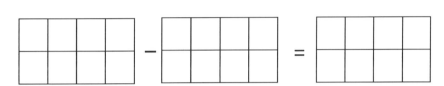

2 Kayla studied for a total of 150 minutes. She spent 50 minutes studying Spanish. What fraction of her total study time did she spend studying Spanish?

Ⓐ $\frac{1}{5}$

Ⓑ $\frac{1}{4}$

Ⓒ $\frac{1}{3}$

Ⓓ $\frac{1}{2}$

3   An orange tree has a height of 2.45 meters. What is the height of the tree in centimeters? Write your answer below.

_____ cm

4   Which diagram represents the sum of $\frac{1}{4}$ and $\frac{1}{8}$?

Ⓐ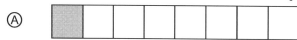

Ⓑ

Ⓒ

Ⓓ

5   Which number is less than 35.052?

    Ⓐ   35.009

    Ⓑ   35.061

    Ⓒ   35.101

    Ⓓ   35.077

6 The table below shows a set of number pairs.

x	y
1	2
3	5
5	9

If the points were plotted on a coordinate grid, which of the following would be the coordinates of one of the points?

Ⓐ   (0, 0)

Ⓑ   (2, 1)

Ⓒ   (3, 5)

Ⓓ   (4, 6)

7 A pattern of numbers is shown below.

8, 13, 18, 23, 28, 33, 38, ...

Circle **all** the numbers that could be numbers in the pattern.

41	53	60	65	67
71	76	88	92	99

8   An orchard has a total of 192 orange trees. They are planted in rows of 12 orange trees each. How many rows of orange trees does the orchard have?

Show your work.

Answer _____

9   Joshua bought a pair of sunglasses for $14.85 and a phone case for $2.55. How much change should he receive from $20?

Show your work.

Answer _____

10   The graph below shows a line segment.

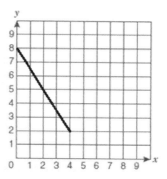

Part A

Complete the table below to show the coordinates of three points the line passes through.

x	0	2	4
y			

Part B

What are the coordinates of the point where the line intercepts the *y*-axis?

Answer _____

11   The model below was made with 1-inch cubes.

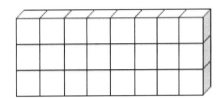

What is the volume of the model? Be sure to include the correct units in your answer.

Show your work.

Answer _____

12 Candice has a painting canvas that is $\frac{3}{4}$ foot long and $\frac{3}{4}$ foot wide. What is the area of the canvas? Shade the diagram below to find the area of the canvas.

Show your work.

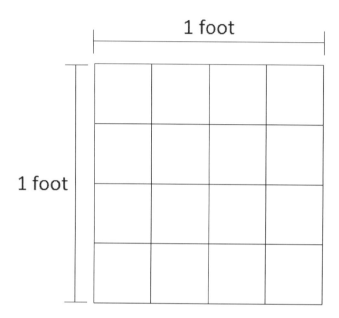

Answer _____ square feet

13   Jasper painted $\frac{1}{2}$ of his room on Saturday. On Sunday, he painted $\frac{1}{3}$ of the remaining part of his room. What fraction of his room does Jasper have left to paint?

Show your work.

Answer _____

14   **Part A**

Shade the model below to show $1\frac{2}{5}$.

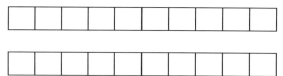

Part B

Use the model to find the value of $1\frac{2}{5} \div 2$.

Answer _____

On the lines below, explain how you found your answer.

_____

_____

_____

_____

_____

15 What are the two smallest 3-digit numbers that can be made using the digits 5, 7, and 2? Each digit must be used only once in each number.

Answer _____ and _____

On the lines below, explain how you found your answer.

_____

_____

_____

_____

_____

END OF SESSION 1

PARCC Performance-Based Assessment

Practice Test 2

Session 2

Instructions

Read each question carefully. For each multiple-choice question, fill in the circle for the correct answer. For other types of questions, follow the directions given in the question.

Some questions may ask you to show your work. Be sure to show your work or explain how you found your answer in the space provided.

You may use a ruler and a protractor to help you answer questions. You may not use a calculator on this test. You may use the information below to help you answer questions.

REFERENCE INFORMATION

1 mile = 5,280 feet
1 mile = 1,760 yards

1 pound = 16 ounces
1 ton = 2,000 pounds

1 cup = 8 fluid ounces
1 pint = 2 cups
1 quart = 2 pints
1 gallon = 4 quarts
1 liter = 1000 cubic centimeters

Right Rectangular Prism $V = Bh$ or $V = lwh$

16 How is the numeral 55.12 written in words?

  Ⓐ   Fifty-five hundred and twelve

  Ⓑ   Fifty-five and twelve thousandths

  Ⓒ   Fifty-five and twelve hundredths

  Ⓓ   Fifty-five and twelve

17 It took James and his family $2\frac{1}{4}$ hours to drive from their house to the beach. How many minutes did the drive take? Write your answer below.

_____ minutes

18 A cat weighs 9 pounds. How many ounces does the cat weigh?

  Ⓐ   36 oz

  Ⓑ   108 oz

  Ⓒ   144 oz

  Ⓓ   72 oz

19 What is the value of 10^3?

    Ⓐ   30

    Ⓑ   100

    Ⓒ   1,000

    Ⓓ   3,000

20 Which pairs of numbers could be added to the table below? Select **all** the correct answers.

Number	Number ÷ 10
85.04	8.504
501.62	50.162
19.483	1.9483

☐ | 28.63 | 286.3 |

☐ | 3.65 | 0.365 |

☐ | 987.78 | 9.8778 |

☐ | 62.69 | 0.6269 |

☐ | 7.25 | 72.5 |

☐ | 46.77 | 4.677 |

21   Which number makes the number sentence below true?

$$2 \div \square = 8$$

Ⓐ $\frac{1}{2}$

Ⓑ $\frac{1}{4}$

Ⓒ $\frac{1}{8}$

Ⓓ $\frac{1}{16}$

22   Lewis scored $\frac{3}{20}$ of the points in a basketball game. How many of the team's 120 points did Lewis score?

Ⓐ   15

Ⓑ   18

Ⓒ   20

Ⓓ   35

23   The grid below represents Roberto's backyard.

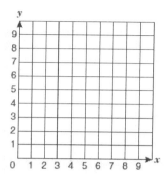

A lemon tree is located at the point (6, 5). An orange tree is located 2 units to the right and 3 units up from the lemon tree. Find the coordinates that represent the location of the orange tree.

Answer _____

Explain how you found your answer.

_____

_____

_____

_____

24   Look at the figure below.

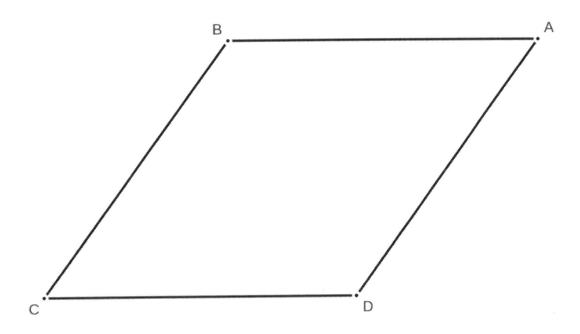

Part A

Identify the two pairs of parallel line segments. Write each line segment on one of the lines below.

Answer _____ and _____, _____ and _____

Part B

Name the shape and describe the properties you used to identify it.

_____

_____

_____

_____

25   The statements below describe quadrilaterals.

At least 1 pair of parallel sides

2 pairs of perpendicular sides

4 equal angles

4 right angles

4 congruent sides

Part A

Circle the statement that correctly describes a trapezoid.

Part B

Which statement above could be used to tell the difference between a rectangle and a square? Explain your answer.

_____

_____

_____

_____

_____

26 A restaurant manager kept a record of the pieces of pie sold one week. He made this list to show the results.

- $\frac{1}{4}$ of the pieces sold were apple pie
- $\frac{3}{8}$ of the pieces sold were pumpkin pie
- $\frac{1}{12}$ of the pieces sold were cherry pie
- The rest of the pieces sold were peach pie.

Part A

What fraction of the pieces sold were peach pie?

Show your work.

Answer _____

Part B

If there were a total of 360 pieces of pie sold that week, how many pieces of cherry pie were sold?

Show your work.

Answer _____

27 Karen made this table to show the amount she spent on lunch each day one week.

Day	Amount
Monday	$5.73
Tuesday	$5.49
Wednesday	$5.51
Thursday	$5.27
Friday	$5.80

What is the total amount Karen spent on lunch that week?

Show your work.

Answer _____

28   Part A

Plot the number 3.8 on the number line below.

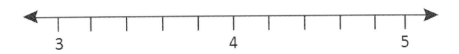

Part B

What is 3.8 rounded to the nearest whole number?

Answer _____

On the lines below, explain how the number line helped you round the number.

_____

_____

_____

_____

29   **Part A**

Circle the measurements that are equivalent to 600 centimeters.

0.6 mm   6 mm   60 mm   6000 mm

0.6 m   6 m   60 m   6000 m

Part B

Convert 600 centimeters to kilometers.

Show your work.

Answer _____ kilometers

30 The model below is made up of 1-centimeter cubes.

Part A

Write and solve an equation to find the volume of the model.

Show your work.

Answer _____ cubic centimeters

Part B

If the height of the model is doubled, how does the volume of the model change? Explain your answer.

_____

_____

_____

_____

END OF SESSION 2

INTRODUCTION TO THE EOY PRACTICE TEST
For Parents, Teachers, and Tutors

About the End-of-Year Assessment

The End-of-Year Assessment (EOY) is taken after about 90% of the school year is complete. It is designed to allow students to demonstrate that they have the skills and knowledge described in the Common Core State Standards. The EOY Assessment only includes the Type I questions described below.

- **Type I** – these items are straightforward selected response or simple computer-based questions. These items are worth 1 or 2 points.

These items may be simple selected response questions where the one correct answer is selected or selected response questions with 2 or more correct answers. The computer-based questions could involve writing numerical answers, sorting or ordering numbers or items, selecting points on a number line or graph, completing number sentences and equations, or using fraction models. This practice test includes a wide range of formats that mimic the computer-based questions.

The actual test contains 36 Type I items. The practice tests in this book contain 50 Type I items. This will ensure that students have practice with all the types of questions they are likely to encounter on the real test and gain the experience needed to complete questions with a range of new formats.

Taking the Test

Just like the real EOY test, the practice test is divided into two sessions. Each session includes 25 questions. On the real test, students are allowed 2 hours to complete each session. To account for the additional questions, students should be allowed 3 hours for each session of the practice test. Students can complete the two sessions on the same day or on different days, but should have a break between sessions.

Calculators and Tools

Students should be provided with a ruler and a protractor to use on both sessions of the test. Students are not allowed to use a calculator on any session of the PARCC tests, and so should complete all the practice tests without the use of a calculator. Students may also use the information on the Reference Sheet included on the first page of the test.

PARCC End-of-Year Assessment

Practice Test 2

Session 1

Instructions

Read each question carefully. For each multiple-choice question, fill in the circle for the correct answer. For other types of questions, follow the directions given in the question.

You may use a ruler and a protractor to help you answer questions. You may not use a calculator on this test. You may use the information below to help you answer questions.

REFERENCE INFORMATION

1 mile = 5,280 feet
1 mile = 1,760 yards

1 pound = 16 ounces
1 ton = 2,000 pounds

1 cup = 8 fluid ounces
1 pint = 2 cups
1 quart = 2 pints
1 gallon = 4 quarts
1 liter = 1000 cubic centimeters

Right Rectangular Prism $V = Bh$ or $V = lwh$

1   The decimal cards for 0.59 and 0.22 are shown below.

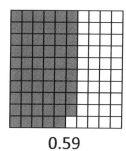   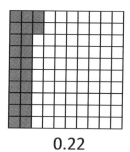

0.59   0.22

What is the difference of 0.59 and 0.22? Write your answer below.

_____

2   Joy made 24 apple pies for a bake sale. Each serving was $\frac{1}{8}$ of a pie. How many servings did Joy make?

Ⓐ   3

Ⓑ   32

Ⓒ   96

Ⓓ   192

3   Look at the fractions below.

$$1\frac{1}{3}, \ 2\frac{1}{2}, \ 3\frac{5}{6}$$

Which procedure can be used to find the sum of the fractions?

Ⓐ   Find the sum of the whole numbers, find the sum of the fractions, and then add the two sums

Ⓑ   Find the sum of the whole numbers, find the sum of the fractions, and then multiply the two sums

Ⓒ   Find the sum of the whole numbers, find the sum of the fractions, and then subtract the two sums

Ⓓ   Find the sum of the whole numbers, find the sum of the fractions, and then divide the two sums

4   Circle **all** the shapes below that ALWAYS have at least one pair of congruent sides.

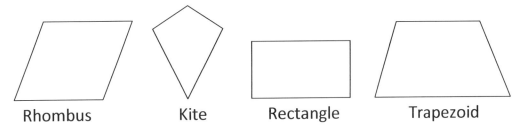

Rhombus   Kite   Rectangle   Trapezoid

5 A diner has 18 tables. Each table can seat 4 people. The diner also has 8 benches that can each seat 6 people. How many people can the diner seat in all?

Ⓐ 36

Ⓑ 120

Ⓒ 260

Ⓓ 308

6 A fraction representing $\frac{6}{8}$ is shown below.

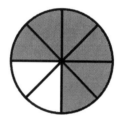

What is the value of $\frac{6}{8} \div 3$?

Ⓐ $\frac{1}{8}$

Ⓑ $\frac{3}{8}$

Ⓒ $\frac{1}{4}$

Ⓓ $\frac{3}{4}$

7   What is the value of the expression below? Write your answer below.

$$42 + 24 \div 3 + 3$$

_____

8   Keegan's family drinks about 2 gallons of milk every 5 days.

About how much milk does Keegan's family drink in 30 days? Give your answer in gallons, quarts, and pints. Write your answers below.

_____ gallons

_____ quarts

_____ pints

9   Chan spent $\frac{3}{8}$ of his total homework time completing his science homework. What calculation could be used to convert the fraction to a decimal?

Ⓐ $3 \div 8 \times 100$

Ⓑ $8 \div 3 \times 100$

Ⓒ $3 \div 8$

Ⓓ $8 \div 3$

10   A recipe for pancakes requires $2\frac{2}{3}$ cups of flour. Donna only has $1\frac{1}{2}$ cups of flour. How many more cups of flour does Donna need?

Ⓐ $\frac{1}{3}$ cup

Ⓑ $\frac{1}{6}$ cup

Ⓒ $1\frac{1}{3}$ cups

Ⓓ $1\frac{1}{6}$ cups

11   There are 6 reams of paper in a box. There are 144 boxes of paper on a pallet. How many reams of paper are on a pallet? Write your answer below.

_____

12   Byron made 9 baskets out of 15 baskets he attempted. What fraction of his baskets did he make? Write the fraction below and then simplify it to lowest terms.

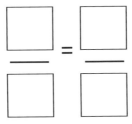

13   The mass of a car is 1.56 tons. What is the mass of the car in pounds?

Ⓐ   312 pounds

Ⓑ   3,120 pounds

Ⓒ   31,200 pounds

Ⓓ   312,000 pounds

14   The table below shows a set of number pairs.

x	y
1	1
3	5
5	9

Which equation shows the relationship between x and y?

Ⓐ $y = x + 2$

Ⓑ $y = x + 4$

Ⓒ $y = 2x - 1$

Ⓓ $y = 3x - 4$

15 Leonard bought 12 tickets to a charity event. The total cost of the tickets was $216. The expression below can be used to find the cost of each ticket.

$$216 \div 12$$

Which of the following is equivalent to the above expression?

Ⓐ $(240 \div 12) + (24 \div 12)$

Ⓑ $(200 \div 10) + (16 \div 2)$

Ⓒ $(216 \div 10) + (216 \div 2)$

Ⓓ $(120 \div 12) + (96 \div 12)$

16 Which terms describe the figure below? Select **all** the correct answers.

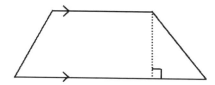

☐   Parallelogram

☐   Polygon

☐   Quadrilateral

☐   Trapezoid

17 Write the coordinates of the points shown on the grid below. Write your answers below.

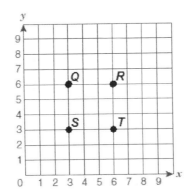

Point *Q*   (___, ___)   Point *R*   (___, ___)

Point *S*   (___, ___)   Point *T*   (___, ___)

18 The table below shows the relationship between the original price and the sale price of a book.

Original price, P	Sale price, S
$10	$7.50
$12	$9
$14	$10.50
$16	$12

What is the rule to find the sale price of a book, in dollars? Add the missing number to the rule below.

$$S = \_\_\_\_ \; P$$

19   Leo measures the length, width, and height of a block. He multiplies the length, width, and height. What is Leo finding?

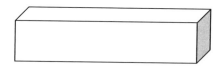

Ⓐ   Surface area

Ⓑ   Mass

Ⓒ   Volume

Ⓓ   Perimeter

20   Circle **all** the figures below that do NOT have any parallel sides.

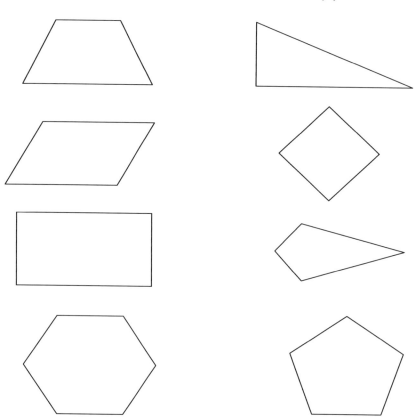

21 The cost of renting a windsurfer is a basic fee of $15 plus an additional $5 for each hour that the windsurfer is rented. Which equation can be used to find c, the cost in dollars of the rental for h hours?

Ⓐ $c = 15h + 5$

Ⓑ $c = 5h + 15$

Ⓒ $c = 15(h + 5)$

Ⓓ $c = 5(h + 15)$

22 The graph below shows the line segment PQ. Point P is at (3, 9). Point Q is at (3, 1).

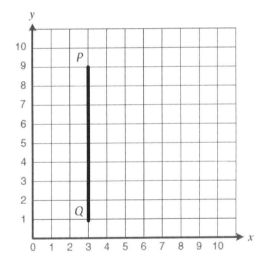

What is the length of the line segment PQ? Write your answer below.

_____ units

23 What decimal is equivalent to the fraction $\frac{33}{100}$?

Ⓐ   0.033

Ⓑ   0.33

Ⓒ   33.0

Ⓓ   3.3

24 Which decimal is represented below?

$$(4 \times 100) + (8 \times 1) + (6 \times \frac{1}{100}) + (3 \times \frac{1}{1000})$$

Ⓐ   480.63

Ⓑ   480.063

Ⓒ   408.63

Ⓓ   408.063

25 If $p = 5$, what is the value of $4(p + 7)$? Write your answer below.

_____

END OF SESSION 1

PARCC End-of-Year Assessment

Practice Test 2

Session 2

Instructions

Read each question carefully. For each multiple-choice question, fill in the circle for the correct answer. For other types of questions, follow the directions given in the question.

You may use a ruler and a protractor to help you answer questions. You may not use a calculator on this test. You may use the information below to help you answer questions.

REFERENCE INFORMATION

1 mile = 5,280 feet
1 mile = 1,760 yards

1 pound = 16 ounces
1 ton = 2,000 pounds

1 cup = 8 fluid ounces
1 pint = 2 cups
1 quart = 2 pints
1 gallon = 4 quarts
1 liter = 1000 cubic centimeters

Right Rectangular Prism $V = Bh$ or $V = lwh$

26   Liam drew a triangle with no equal side lengths, as shown below.

What type of triangle did Liam draw?

Ⓐ   Scalene

Ⓑ   Equilateral

Ⓒ   Isosceles

Ⓓ   Right

27   The table below shows the total number of lemons in different numbers of bags of lemons.

Number of Bags (B)	Number of Lemons (L)
2	16
3	24
5	40
8	64

What is the relationship between the total number of lemons, L, and the number of bags of lemons, B? Complete the equation below to show the relationship.

$$L = \underline{\quad} B$$

28 Amy ordered 3 pizzas for \$6.95 each. She also bought a soft drink for \$1.95. Which equation can be used to find how much change, c, she should receive from \$30?

Ⓐ $c = 30 - 3(6.95 + 1.95)$

Ⓑ $c = 30 - 3(6.95 - 1.95)$

Ⓒ $c = 30 - 6.95 - 1.95$

Ⓓ $c = 30 - (6.95 \times 3) - 1.95$

29 What is the decimal 55.146 rounded to the nearest whole number, nearest tenth, and nearest hundredth? Write your answers below.

Nearest whole number _____

Nearest tenth _____

Nearest hundredth _____

30 What is the value of the expression below? Write your answer below.

$$28 + 4 \div 2 + (9 - 5)$$

_____

31   The table shows the side length of a rhombus and the perimeter of a rhombus.

Side Length, x (cm)	Perimeter, y (cm)
1	4
2	8
3	12
4	16

Which equation represents the relationship between side length and perimeter?

Ⓐ $y = x + 3$

Ⓑ $y = 4x$

Ⓒ $x = y + 4$

Ⓓ $x = 4y$

32   A florist sells balloons in sets of 6. A customer ordered several sets of 6 balloons. Which of these could be the total number of balloons ordered? Circle **all** the correct possible answers.

48   50   54   58   62

66   70   78   80   88

33 The table shows the amount of Don's phone bill for four different months.

Month	Amount
April	$12.22
May	$12.09
June	$12.18
July	$12.05

Place the months in order from the lowest bill to the highest bill. Write the months on the lines below.

Lowest _____

_____

_____

Highest _____

34 Marcus sold drinks at a lemonade stand. The table shows how many drinks of each size he sold.

Size	Number Sold
Small	15
Medium	20
Large	5
Extra large	10

Which size drink made up $\frac{3}{10}$ of the total sold? Write your answer below.

_____

35   What is the rule to find the value of a term in the sequence below?

Position, *n*	Value of Term
1	3
2	5
3	7
4	9

Ⓐ $4n - 4$

Ⓑ $3n$

Ⓒ $2n + 1$

Ⓓ $n + 2$

36   The table shows the amount of rainfall for the first five days of May.

Date	1st	2nd	3rd	4th	5th
Rainfall (cm)	4.59	4.18	4.50	4.61	4.73

Compare the five decimals. Write the decimals on the lines below.

_____ < _____ < _____ < _____ < _____

37   What value of *x* makes the equation below true? Write your answer below.

$$54 \div x = 9$$

x = _____

38   The grid below represents 4 x 7.

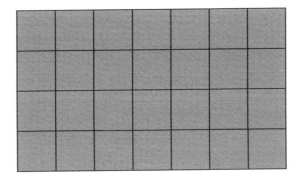

Which of these is another way to represent 4 x 7? Select **all** the correct answers.

☐ 7×4

☐ $7 + 7 + 7 + 7$

☐ $7 + 7 + 7 + 7 + 7 + 7 + 7$

☐ $4 + 4 + 4 + 4$

☐ $4 \times 4 \times 4 \times 4$

☐ $4 + 4 + 4 + 4 + 4 + 4 + 4$

39 Sandy has 129 dimes. Marvin has 185 dimes. What is the total value of Sandy and Marvin's dimes?

Ⓐ $3.04

Ⓑ $3.14

Ⓒ $30.40

Ⓓ $31.40

40 Which of the following is a correct definition of a square?

Ⓐ   A rectangle with two pairs of parallel sides

Ⓑ   A rectangle with adjacent sides perpendicular

Ⓒ   A rhombus with four equal sides

Ⓓ   A rhombus with four right angles

41 Ellen multiplies the number 3 by a fraction. The result is a number greater than 3. Which of these could be the fraction?

Ⓐ $1\frac{1}{4}$

Ⓑ $\frac{8}{9}$

Ⓒ $\frac{1}{6}$

Ⓓ $\frac{1}{2}$

42 Look at the two sequences of numbers below.

First sequence: 0, 4, 8, 12, 16, 20, 24, ...
Second sequence: 0, 8, 16, 24, 32, 40, 48, ...

If the 100th term in the first sequence is represented as n, which of these gives the 100th term in the second sequence?

Ⓐ $n + 4$

Ⓑ $n + 8$

Ⓒ $2n$

Ⓓ $2n + 4$

43 Lloyd bought 4 T-shirts. Each T-shirt cost $7. Which is one way to work out how much change Lloyd would receive from $30?

Ⓐ   Add 4 to 7 and subtract the result from 30

Ⓑ   Add 4 to 7 and add the result to 30

Ⓒ   Multiply 4 by 7 and add the result to 30

Ⓓ   Multiply 4 by 7 and subtract the result from 30

44 An Italian restaurant sells four types of meals. The owner made this table to show how many meals of each type were sold one night. According to the table, which statements are true? Select **all** the correct statements.

Meal	Number Sold
Pasta	16
Pizza	18
Salad	11
Risotto	9

☐ The store sold more pizza meals than salad and risotto meals combined.

☐ The store sold twice as many pizza meals as risotto meals.

☐ The store sold more pasta meals than any other type of meal.

☐ The store sold half as many salad meals as pasta meals.

☐ The store sold over 50 meals in total.

45 Jordan is putting CDs in a case. She can fit 24 CDs in each row. She has 120 CDs. Which equation can be used to find the total number of rows, r, she can fill?

Ⓐ $r \times 120 = 24$

Ⓑ $r \div 24 = 120$

Ⓒ $120 \times 24 = r$

Ⓓ $120 \div 24 = r$

46   Jay made 8 trays of 6 muffins each.

He gave 12 muffins away. He packed the remaining muffins in bags of 4 muffins each. Which expression can be used to find how many bags of muffins he packed?

Ⓐ $(8 \times 6) - 12 \div 4$

Ⓑ $(8 \times 6) - (12 \div 4)$

Ⓒ $8 \times (6 - 12 \div 4)$

Ⓓ $(8 \times 6 - 12) \div 4$

47   The table shows the side length of an equilateral triangle and the perimeter of an equilateral triangle.

Side Length, *l* (inches)	Perimeter, *P* (inches)
2	6
3	9
4	12
5	15

Which equation represents the relationship between side length and perimeter?

Ⓐ $P = l + 4$

Ⓑ $P = 3l$

Ⓒ $l = P + 4$

Ⓓ $l = 3P$

48 Which term describes the triangle below?

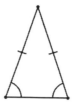

    Ⓐ   Isosceles

    Ⓑ   Scalene

    Ⓒ   Equilateral

    Ⓓ   Right

49 Complete the missing numbers to write 600,000 in three more different ways.

6,000   hundreds

_____ thousands

_____ ten-thousands

_____ hundred-thousands

50 Which statement is true about the product of $\frac{1}{3}$ and 6?

    Ⓐ   The product is greater than 6.

    Ⓑ   The product is less than $\frac{1}{3}$.

    Ⓒ   The product is a value between the two factors.

    Ⓓ   The product is a value equal to one of the factors.

END OF SESSION 2

ANSWER KEY

Common Core State Standards

The *Massachusetts Curriculum Frameworks* describe the skills that students are expected to have. These frameworks are based on the Common Core State Standards. They incorporate all the Common Core standards, as well as some additional skills. Just like the real PARCC assessments, the questions in this book test whether students have the knowledge and skills described in the Common Core State Standards.

Assessing Skills and Knowledge

The skills listed in the Common Core State Standards are divided into five topics, or clusters. These are:

- Operations and Algebraic Thinking
- Number and Operations in Base Ten
- Number and Operations – Fractions
- Measurement and Data
- Geometry

The answer key identifies the topic for each question. Use the topics listed to identify general areas of strength and weakness. Then target revision and instruction accordingly.

The answer key also identifies the specific math skill that each question is testing. Use the skills listed to identify skills that the student is lacking. Then target revision and instruction accordingly.

Scoring Constructed Response Questions

This practice test book includes constructed response questions, where students provide a written answer to a question or complete a task. These questions are often scored based on the final answer given as well as the work shown. When asked to show work, students may show calculations, use diagrams, or explain their thinking or process in words. Any form of work that shows the student's understanding can be accepted. Other questions are scored based on tasks completed, explanations given, or justifications given. Answers are provided for these questions, as well as guidance on how to score the questions.

PARCC Performance-Based Assessment, Practice Test 1, Session 1

Question	Answer	Topic	Common Core Skill
1	A	Number & Operations in Base Ten	Perform operations with multi-digit whole numbers.
2	D	Geometry	Represent real world and mathematical problems by graphing points in the first quadrant of the coordinate plane, and interpret coordinate values of points in the context of the situation.
3	B	Number & Operations-Fractions	Interpret a fraction as division of the numerator by the denominator.
4	triangle square pentagon hexagon octagon	Geometry	Classify two-dimensional figures in a hierarchy based on properties.
5	6	Number & Operations in Base Ten	Find whole-number quotients of whole numbers with up to four-digit dividends and two-digit divisors, using strategies based on properties of operations.
6	$65 \div 5 = 13$	Number & Operations in Base Ten	Find whole-number quotients of whole numbers. Illustrate and explain the calculation by using equations, rectangular arrays, and/or area models.
7	C	Operations/Algebraic Thinking	Write simple expressions that record calculations with numbers, and interpret numerical expressions without evaluating them.
8	See Below	Number & Operations in Base Ten	Perform operations with multi-digit whole numbers. Fluently multiply multi-digit whole numbers using the standard algorithm.
9	See Below	Operations/Algebraic Thinking	Use parentheses, brackets, or braces in numerical expressions, and evaluate expressions with these symbols.
10	See Below	Measurement & Data	Convert among different-sized standard measurement units within a given measurement system, and use these conversions in solving multi-step, real world problems.
11	See Below	Number & Operations-Fractions	Solve word problems involving division of whole numbers leading to answers in the form of fractions or mixed numbers, e.g., by using visual fraction models or equations to represent the problem.
12	See Below	Number & Operations in Base Ten	Add, subtract, multiply, and divide decimals to hundredths.
13	See Below	Number & Operations in Base Ten	Add, subtract, multiply, and divide decimals to hundredths.
14	See Below	Geometry	Represent real world and mathematical problems by graphing points in the first quadrant of the coordinate plane, and interpret coordinate values of points in the context of the situation.
15	See Below	Geometry	Classify two-dimensional figures in a hierarchy based on properties.

Q8.
Answer
33

Work
The work should show the calculation of $(48 \times 7) - 303 = 33$.

Scoring Information
Give a total score out of 3.
Give a score of 1 for the correct answer.
Give a score out of 2 for the working.

Q9.
Answer
34

Work
The work should show the following steps.
$(16 + 20) - 8 \div 4 \rightarrow (36) - 8 \div 4 \rightarrow (36) - 2 \rightarrow 34$

Scoring Information
Give a total score out of 3.
Give a score of 1 for the correct answer.
Give a score out of 2 for the working.

Q10.
Answer
5 pints

Work
The work should show the conversion of 3 quarts to 6 pints, and then the subtraction of 1 pint.

Scoring Information
Give a total score out of 3.
Give a score of 1 for the correct answer.
Give a score out of 2 for the working.

Q11.
Answer
$6\frac{1}{4}$ minutes

Work
The work may show a numerical calculation of $100 \div 16$, or may use the grid to divide 100 into 16 segments with 4 squares remaining or groups of 16 segments with 4 squares remaining.

Scoring Information
Give a total score out of 4.
Give a score of 1 for the correct answer.
Give a score out of 3 for the working.

Q12.
Answer
973.2 miles

Work
The work should show the calculation of 8192.6 − 7219.4 = 973.2.

Scoring Information
Give a total score out of 3.
Give a score of 1 for the correct answer.
Give a score out of 2 for the working.

Q13.
Answer
$0.55 or 55 cents

Work
The work should show the calculation of (1.85 + 0.95) − 2.25 = 0.55.

Scoring Information
Give a total score out of 3.
Give a score of 1 for the correct answer.
Give a score out of 2 for the working.

Q14.
Answer
(9, 1)

Explanation
The student may describe the calculation (5 + 4, 4 − 3) = (9, 1), or may describe plotting the new point on the grid and reading the coordinates.

Scoring Information
Give a total score out of 3.
Give a score of 1 for the correct answer.
Give a score out of 2 for the explanation.

Q15.
Answer
isosceles

Explanation
The student should explain that the triangle has two sides of equal length and one side of a different length.

Scoring Information
Give a total score out of 3.
Give a score of 1 for the correct answer.
Give a score out of 2 for the explanation.

PARCC Performance-Based Assessment, Practice Test 1, Session 2

Question	Answer	Topic	Common Core Skill
16	$C = 3d$	Operations/Algebraic Thinking	Analyze patterns and relationships by identifying apparent relationships between corresponding terms.
17	A	Geometry	Classify two-dimensional figures in a hierarchy based on properties.
18	D	Number & Operations-Fractions	Solve word problems involving addition and subtraction of fractions referring to the same whole, including cases of unlike denominators, e.g., by using visual fraction models or equations to represent the problem.
19	C	Number & Operations in Base Ten	Add, subtract, multiply, and divide decimals to hundredths.
20	D	Operations/Algebraic Thinking	Use parentheses, brackets, or braces in numerical expressions, and evaluate expressions with these symbols.
21	D	Operations/Algebraic Thinking	Write simple expressions that record calculations with numbers, and interpret numerical expressions without evaluating them.
22	$53\frac{1}{3}$ yards	Measurement & Data	Convert among different-sized standard measurement units within a given measurement system, and use these conversions in solving multi-step, real world problems.
23	See Below	Operations/Algebraic Thinking	Generate two numerical patterns using two given rules. Identify apparent relationships between corresponding terms.
24	See Below	Measurement & Data	Make a line plot to display a data set of measurements in fractions of a unit (1/2, 1/4, 1/8). Use operations on fractions for this grade to solve problems involving information presented in line plots.
25	See Below	Number & Operations in Base Ten	Find whole-number quotients of whole numbers with up to four-digit dividends and two-digit divisors, using strategies based on place value, the properties of operations, and/or the relationship between multiplication and division. Illustrate and explain the calculation by using equations, rectangular arrays, and/or area models.
26	See Below	Number & Operations in Base Ten	Add, subtract, multiply, and divide decimals to hundredths, using concrete models or drawings and strategies based on place value, properties of operations, and/or the relationship between addition and subtraction; relate the strategy to a written method and explain the reasoning used.
27	See Below	Measurement & Data	Measure volumes by counting unit cubes, using cubic cm, cubic in, cubic ft, and improvised units.
28	See Below	Geometry	Use a pair of perpendicular number lines, called axes, to define a coordinate system, with the intersection of the lines (the origin) arranged to coincide with the 0 on each line and a given point in the plane located by using an ordered pair of numbers, called its coordinates.
29	See Below	Operations/Algebraic Thinking	Use parentheses, brackets, or braces in numerical expressions, and evaluate expressions with these symbols.
30	See Below	Number & Operations-Fractions	Apply and extend previous understandings of multiplication to multiply a fraction or whole number by a fraction.

Q23.
Part A
The student should complete the table with the following values:

Harris's Total Savings	3	6	9	12	15	18
Jamie's Total Savings	6	12	18	24	30	36

Part B
The student should explain that Jamie's total savings are always twice Harris's total savings.

Scoring Information
Give a total score out of 6.
Give a score out of 2 for the values for Harris's Total Savings in Part A.
Give a score out of 2 for the values for Jamie's Total Savings in Part A.
Give a score out of 2 for the explanation in Part B.

Q24.
Part A
The work should show the completed graph as below.

Hailstone Diameter (inches)

```
              X
              X                 X       X
              X       X         X       X       X       X
  ───────────────────────────────────────────────────────────
      0      1/8     1/4    3/8    1/2    5/8    3/4    7/8     1
```

Part B
Answer
$\frac{1}{2}$ inch

Explanation
The student should describe using the line plot to find the middle value.

Scoring Information
Give a total score out of 6.
Give a score out of 3 for the line plot created in Part A.
Give a score of 1 for the correct answer to Part B.
Give a score out of 2 for the explanation in Part B.

Q25.
Part A
$448 = 32h$

Part B
Answer
$14

Work
The work should show solving the equation $448 = 32h$ to find $h = 14$.

Scoring Information
Give a total score out of 4.
Give a score of 1 for the correct answer to Part A.
Give a score of 1 for the correct answer to Part B.
Give a score out of 2 for the working.

Q26.
Answer
0.8 miles

Explanation
The student should describe shading 2.6 on the diagram, shading 1.8 on the diagram, and finding the number of squares shaded only by 2.6. A sample completed diagram is shown below.

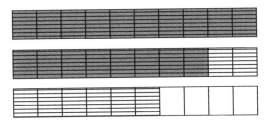

Scoring Information
Give a total score out of 4.
Give a score out of 1 for using the diagram to represent the decimals.
Give a score of 1 for the correct answer.
Give a score out of 2 for the explanation.

Q27.
Answer
60 cubic centimeters

Work
The work could show the calculation 3 × 4 × 5 = 60, or could show calculating 20 cubes in each row and 3 rows of cubes.

Scoring Information
Give a total score out of 3.
Give a score of 1 for the correct answer.
Give a score out of 2 for the working.

Q28.
Answer
(2, 4)

Work
The work should show an understanding that the origin is the point (0, 0) and that the star at (2, 4) is closest to the origin. The student may draw lines to show the distance to each star, or could explain that the closest star is 2 units to the right of the origin and 4 units up from the origin.

Scoring Information
Give a total score out of 3.
Give a score of 1 for the correct answer.
Give a score out of 2 for the working.

Q29.
Part A
$(4 \times 3) + (5 \times 7)$

Part B
Answer
$47

Work
The work should show simplifying the expression as below.
$(4 \times 3) + (5 \times 7)$
12 + 35
47

Scoring Information
Give a total score out of 4.
Give a score of 1 for the correct expression in Part A.
Give a score of 1 for the correct answer in Part B.
Give a score out of 2 for the working.

Q30.
Answer
80

Work
The work could show the calculation of $200 \times \frac{2}{5} = 80$. The work could also show a two-step process of dividing 200 by 5 to find one-fifth and then multiplying the result by 2 to find two-fifths.

Scoring Information
Give a total score out of 3.
Give a score of 1 for the correct answer.
Give a score out of 2 for the working.

PARCC End-Of-Year Assessment, Practice Test 1, Session 1

Question	Answer	Topic	Common Core Skill
1	70	Number & Operations-Fractions	Add and subtract fractions with unlike denominators (including mixed numbers) by replacing given fractions with equivalent fractions in such a way as to produce an equivalent sum or difference of fractions with like denominators.
2	D	Number & Operations-Fractions	Solve real world problems involving division of fractions by whole numbers, e.g., by using visual fraction models and equations to represent the problem.
3	$4.70	Number & Operations in Base Ten	Add, subtract, multiply, and divide decimals to hundredths.
4	A	Number & Operations in Base Ten	Add, subtract, multiply, and divide decimals to hundredths.
5	D	Number & Operations in Base Ten	Fluently multiply multi-digit whole numbers using the standard algorithm.
6	C	Number & Operations-Fractions	Interpret a fraction as division of the numerator by the denominator.
7	(4, 9) (6, 7)	Geometry	Locate a point in a coordinate system by using an ordered pair of numbers, called its coordinates.
8	B	Number & Operations in Base Ten	Explain patterns in the placement of the decimal point when a decimal is multiplied or divided by a power of 10.
9	B	Number & Operations-Fractions	Add and subtract fractions with unlike denominators (including mixed numbers) by replacing given fractions with equivalent fractions in such a way as to produce an equivalent sum or difference of fractions with like denominators.
10	$8, $14, $16	Number & Operations in Base Ten	Find whole-number quotients of whole numbers with up to four-digit dividends and two-digit divisors, using strategies based on place value, the properties of operations, and/or the relationship between multiplication and division.
11	C	Number & Operations in Base Ten	Add, subtract, multiply, and divide decimals to hundredths.
12	(3, 6) (9, 6) (9, 2) (7, 2)	Geometry	Locate a point in a coordinate system by using an ordered pair of numbers, called its coordinates.
13	$31.40	Number & Operations in Base Ten	Add, subtract, multiply, and divide decimals to hundredths.
14	D	Measurement & Data	Convert among different-sized standard measurement units within a given measurement system, and use these conversions in solving multi-step, real world problems.
15	D	Measurement & Data	Recognize volume as an attribute of solid figures and understand concepts of volume measurement.
16	10 hours	Measurement & Data	Make a line plot to display a data set of measurements in fractions of a unit (1/2, 1/4, 1/8). Use operations on fractions for this grade to solve problems involving information presented in line plots.

17	A	Geometry	Use a coordinate system and understand that the first number indicates how far to travel from the origin in the direction of one axis, and the second number indicates how far to travel in the direction of the second axis.
18	4 pounds 64 ounces	Measurement & Data	Convert among different-sized standard measurement units within a given measurement system, and use these conversions in solving multi-step, real world problems.
19	$2 \times 3 \times 12 = 72$ cm^3	Measurement & Data	Relate volume to the operations of multiplication and addition and solve real world and mathematical problems involving volume.
20	C	Number & Operations in Base Ten	Read and write decimals to thousandths using base-ten numerals, number names, and expanded form.
21	128	Measurement & Data	Convert among different-sized standard measurement units within a given measurement system, and use these conversions in solving multi-step, real world problems.
22	C	Measurement & Data	Convert among different-sized standard measurement units within a given measurement system, and use these conversions in solving multi-step, real world problems.
23	B	Measurement & Data	Measure volumes by counting unit cubes, using cubic cm, cubic in, cubic ft, and improvised units.
24	A	Operations/Algebraic Thinking	Generate two numerical patterns using two given rules. Identify apparent relationships between corresponding terms.
25	C	Operations/Algebraic Thinking	Form ordered pairs consisting of corresponding terms from the two patterns, and graph the ordered pairs on a coordinate plane.

PARCC End-Of-Year Assessment, Practice Test 1, Session 2

Question	Answer	Topic	Common Core Skill
26	3^3 $3 \times 3 \times 3$	Measurement & Data	Relate volume to the operations of multiplication and addition and solve real world and mathematical problems involving volume.
27	60 baseball cards	Number & Operations in Base Ten	Perform operations with multi-digit whole numbers.
28	C	Geometry	Locate a point in a coordinate system by using an ordered pair of numbers, called its coordinates.
29	Parallelogram Quadrilateral	Geometry	Classify two-dimensional figures in a hierarchy based on properties.
30	B	Operations/Algebraic Thinking	Analyze patterns and relationships by identifying apparent relationships between corresponding terms.
31	C	Operations/Algebraic Thinking	Write simple expressions that record calculations with numbers, and interpret numerical expressions without evaluating them.
32	9 feet 108 inches	Measurement & Data	Convert among different-sized standard measurement units within a given measurement system, and use these conversions in solving multi-step, real world problems.
33	B	Operations/Algebraic Thinking	Use parentheses, brackets, or braces in numerical expressions, and evaluate expressions with these symbols.
34	35.682 63.543	Number & Operations in Base Ten	Use place value understanding to round decimals to any place.
35	24 cubic units	Measurement & Data	Measure volumes by counting unit cubes, using cubic cm, cubic in, cubic ft, and improvised units.
36	x 3 5 7 y 1 3 5	Operations/Algebraic Thinking	Form ordered pairs consisting of corresponding terms from the two patterns, and graph the ordered pairs on a coordinate plane.
37	C	Operations/Algebraic Thinking	Write simple expressions that record calculations with numbers, and interpret numerical expressions without evaluating them.
38	B	Number & Operations in Base Ten	Read and write decimals to thousandths using base-ten numerals, number names, and expanded form.
39	1.06	Number & Operations in Base Ten	Explain patterns in the placement of the decimal point when a decimal is multiplied or divided by a power of 10.
40	D	Measurement & Data	Apply the formulas $V = l \times w \times h$ and $V = b \times h$ for rectangular prisms to find volumes of right rectangular prisms with whole-number edge lengths in the context of solving real world and mathematical problems.
41	C	Operations/Algebraic Thinking	Analyze patterns and relationships.
42	$8	Number & Operations in Base Ten	Perform operations with multi-digit whole numbers.

43	C	Number & Operations-Fractions	Add and subtract fractions with unlike denominators (including mixed numbers) by replacing given fractions with equivalent fractions in such a way as to produce an equivalent sum or difference of fractions with like denominators.
44	C	Operations/Algebraic Thinking	Use parentheses, brackets, or braces in numerical expressions, and evaluate expressions with these symbols.
45	5 of the 8 squares shaded	Number & Operations-Fractions	Solve word problems involving addition and subtraction of fractions referring to the same whole, including cases of unlike denominators, e.g., by using visual fraction models or equations to represent the problem.
46	A	Measurement & Data	Convert among different-sized standard measurement units within a given measurement system, and use these conversions in solving multi-step, real world problems.
47	B	Operations/Algebraic Thinking	Write simple expressions that record calculations with numbers, and interpret numerical expressions without evaluating them.
48	D	Operations/Algebraic Thinking	Write simple expressions that record calculations with numbers, and interpret numerical expressions without evaluating them.
49	B	Number & Operations-Fractions	Find the area of a rectangle with fractional side lengths by tiling it with unit squares of the appropriate unit fraction side lengths, and show that the area is the same as would be found by multiplying the side lengths. Multiply fractional side lengths to find areas of rectangles, and represent fraction products as rectangular areas.
50	B	Geometry	Understand that attributes belonging to a category of two-dimensional figures also belong to all subcategories of that category.

PARCC Performance-Based Assessment, Practice Test 2, Session 1

Question	Answer	Topic	Common Core Skill
1	$\frac{3}{8}$	Number & Operations-Fractions	Solve word problems involving addition and subtraction of fractions referring to the same whole, including cases of unlike denominators, e.g., by using visual fraction models or equations to represent the problem.
2	C	Number & Operations-Fractions	Solve word problems involving division of whole numbers leading to answers in the form of fractions or mixed numbers, e.g., by using visual fraction models or equations to represent the problem.
3	245 cm	Measurement & Data	Convert among different-sized standard measurement units within a given measurement system, and use these conversions in solving multi-step, real world problems.
4	B	Number & Operations-Fractions	Add and subtract fractions with unlike denominators.
5	A	Number & Operations in Base Ten	Compare two decimals to thousandths based on meanings of the digits in each place, using >, =, and < symbols to record the results of comparisons.
6	C	Operations/Algebraic Thinking	Form ordered pairs consisting of corresponding terms from the two patterns, and graph the ordered pairs on a coordinate plane.
7	53, 88	Operations/Algebraic Thinking	Analyze patterns and relationships by identifying apparent relationships between corresponding terms.
8	See Below	Number & Operations in Base Ten	Find whole-number quotients of whole numbers with up to four-digit dividends and two-digit divisors, using strategies based on place value, the properties of operations, and/or the relationship between multiplication and division.
9	See Below	Number & Operations in Base Ten	Add, subtract, multiply, and divide decimals to hundredths.
10	See Below	Geometry	Locate a point in a coordinate system by using an ordered pair of numbers, called its coordinates. Understand the convention that the names of the two axes and the coordinates correspond (e.g., x-axis and x-coordinate, y-axis and y-coordinate).
11	See Below	Measurement & Data	Measure volumes by counting unit cubes, using cubic cm, cubic in, cubic ft, and improvised units.
12	See Below	Number & Operations-Fractions	Find the area of a rectangle with fractional side lengths by tiling it with unit squares of the appropriate unit fraction side lengths, and show that the area is the same as would be found by multiplying the side lengths. Multiply fractional side lengths to find areas of rectangles, and represent fraction products as rectangular areas.
13	See Below	Number & Operations-Fractions	Apply and extend previous understandings of multiplication to multiply a fraction or whole number by a fraction.
14	See Below	Number & Operations-Fractions	Apply and extend previous understandings of division to divide unit fractions by whole numbers and whole numbers by unit fractions.
15	See Below	Number & Operations in Base Ten	Recognize that in a multi-digit number, a digit in one place represents 10 times as much as it represents in the place to its right and 1/10 of what it represents in the place to its left.

Q8.
Answer
16

Work
The work may show the calculation of 192 ÷ 12 = 16. The work could also show a diagram representing 16 rows of 12.

Scoring Information
Give a total score out of 3.
Give a score of 1 for the correct answer.
Give a score out of 2 for the working.

Q9.
Answer
$2.60

Work
The work could show the calculation of 20 – (14.85 + 2.55) = 2.60 or could show the two-step subtraction of 20 – 14.85 = 5.15 and 5.15 – 2.55 = 2.60.

Scoring Information
Give a total score out of 3.
Give a score of 1 for the correct answer.
Give a score out of 2 for the working.

Q10.
Part A
The student should complete the table as shown below.

x	0	2	4
y	8	5	2

Part B
Answer
(0, 8)

Scoring Information
Give a total score out of 4.
Give a score of 1 for each correct value added to the table in Part A.
Give a score of 1 for the correct answer to Part B.

Q11.
Answer
24 cubic inches or 24 in^3

Work
The work may show the calculation of 8 × 3 × 1 = 24 or could show that the student counted the cubes.

Scoring Information
Give a total score out of 3.
Give a score of 1 for the correct numerical answer.
Give a score of 1 for the correct units.
Give a score out of 1 for the working.

Q12.
Answer
$\frac{9}{16}$ square feet

Work
The diagram should be shaded to show a 3 × 3 section, as shown. The student should recognize that 9 out of 16 squares are shaded, so the area is $\frac{9}{16}$ square feet.

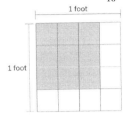

Scoring Information
Give a total score out of 4.
Give a score of 1 for the correct answer.
Give a score of 1 for shading the diagram correctly.
Give a score out of 2 for the working.

Q13.
Answer
$\frac{1}{3}$

Work
The student may find the area painted on the two days as $\frac{1}{2}$ and $\frac{1}{2} \times \frac{1}{3} = \frac{1}{6}$, and then find the remaining area by calculating $1 - \frac{1}{2} - \frac{1}{6} = \frac{2}{3}$. The student may also use a diagram such as the one below to find the area remaining.

Day 1	Day 1	Day 1
Day 2	Day 3	Day 3

Scoring Information
Give a total score out of 3.
Give a score of 1 for the correct answer.
Give a score out of 2 for the working.

Q14.
Part A
The model should have 14 squares shaded.

Part *B*
Answer
$\frac{7}{10}$

Explanation
The student should describe using half of the shaded squares to represent $1\frac{2}{5} \div 2$, and seeing on the diagram that this is equal to 7 of the 10 squares. The student could also describe adding half of the whole number 1 to half of the fraction $\frac{2}{5}$.

Scoring Information
Give a total score out of 4.
Give a score of 1 for the correct shading in Part A.
Give a score of 1 for the correct answer in Part B.
Give a score out of 2 for the explanation.

Q15.
Answer
257 and 275

Explanation
The explanation should refer to the place value of the numbers. It may describe how the number with the lowest value should be in the hundreds place.

Scoring Information
Give a total score out of 4.
Give a score of 1 for each correct number.
Give a score out of 2 for the explanation.

PARCC Performance-Based Assessment, Practice Test 2, Session 2

Question	Answer	Topic	Common Core Skill
16	C	Number & Operations in Base Ten	Read and write decimals to thousandths using base-ten numerals, number names, and expanded form.
17	135 minutes	Number & Operations-Fractions	Solve real world problems involving multiplication of fractions and mixed numbers.
18	C	Measurement & Data	Convert among different-sized standard measurement units within a given measurement system, and use these conversions in solving multi-step, real world problems.
19	C	Number & Operations in Base Ten	Use whole-number exponents to denote powers of 10.
20	3.65, 0.365 46.77, 4.677	Number & Operations in Base Ten	Explain patterns in the placement of the decimal point when a decimal is multiplied or divided by a power of 10.
21	B	Number & Operations-Fractions	Interpret division of a whole number by a unit fraction, and compute such quotients.
22	B	Number & Operations-Fractions	Apply and extend previous understandings of multiplication to multiply a whole number by a fraction.
23	See Below	Geometry	Represent real world and mathematical problems by graphing points in the first quadrant of the coordinate plane, and interpret coordinate values of points in the context of the situation.
24	See Below	Geometry	Understand that attributes belonging to a category of two-dimensional figures also belong to all subcategories of that category.
25	See Below	Geometry	Classify two-dimensional figures in a hierarchy based on properties.
26	See Below	Number & Operations-Fractions	Solve word problems involving addition and subtraction of fractions referring to the same whole, including cases of unlike denominators. Apply and extend previous understandings of multiplication to multiply a fraction or whole number by a fraction.
27	See Below	Number & Operations in Base Ten	Add, subtract, multiply, and divide decimals to hundredths, using strategies based on place value and properties of operations.
28	See Below	Number & Operations in Base Ten	Use place value understanding to round decimals to any place.
29	See Below	Measurement & Data	Convert among different-sized standard measurement units within a given measurement system, and use these conversions in solving multi-step, real world problems.
30	See Below	Measurement & Data	Relate volume to the operations of multiplication and addition and solve real world and mathematical problems involving volume.

Q23.
Answer
(8, 8)

Explanation
The student may describe the calculation (6 + 2, 5 + 3) = (8, 8), or may describe plotting the new point on the grid and reading the coordinates.

Scoring Information
Give a total score out of 3.
Give a score of 1 for the correct answer.
Give a score out of 2 for the explanation.

Q24.
Part A
Answer
BA and CD, BC and AD

Part B
The student should identify that the shape is a rhombus. The explanation should refer to the two pairs of parallel sides and the four sides being equal in length. The explanation may also include that the shape is not a square because the angles are not right angles.

Scoring Information
Give a total score out of 4.
Give a score of 0.5 for each correct pair listed in Part A.
Give a score of 1 for the correct shape identified in Part B.
Give a score out of 2 for the explanation in Part B.

Q25.
Part A
Answer
The student should circle the following statement.
At least 1 pair of parallel sides

Part B
Answer
The student should identify that 4 congruent sides could be used to tell the difference between a rectangle and a square. The answer should show an understanding that all the statements are true for both rectangles and squares except that a square has 4 congruent sides and a rectangle does not.

Scoring Information
Give a total score out of 4.
Give a score of 1 for the correct statement circled in Part A.
Give a score of 1 for identifying the correct statement in Part B.
Give a score out of 2 for the explanation in Part B.

Q26.
Part A
Answer

$$\frac{7}{24}$$

Work

The student may add the three fractions to find $\frac{17}{24}$ and then calculate $1 - \frac{17}{24} = \frac{7}{24}$. The student may convert all the fractions, and then calculate $\frac{24}{24} - \frac{6}{24} - \frac{9}{24} - \frac{2}{24} = \frac{7}{24}$. The student could also use a diagram to find the remaining fraction, such as the one below.

Pumpkin	Pumpkin	Pumpkin	Apple	Apple	Apple
Pumpkin	Pumpkin	Pumpkin	Apple	Apple	Apple
Pumpkin	Pumpkin	Pumpkin	Peach	Peach	Peach
Cherry	Cherry	Peach	Peach	Peach	Peach

Part B
Answer

30

Work

The work should show the calculation of $360 \times \frac{1}{12} = 30$. The work could show an understanding that $360 \times \frac{1}{12}$ is the same as $\frac{360}{12}$ or $360 \div 12$.

Scoring Information

Give a total score out of 6.
Give a score of 1 for the correct answer to Part A.
Give a score out of 2 for the working in Part A.
Give a score of 1 for the correct answer to Part B.
Give a score out of 2 for the working in Part B.

Q27.
Answer

$27.80

Work

The work should show the calculation of 5.73 + 5.49 + 5.51 + 5.27 + 5.80 = 27.80. The student could also complete the additions in steps by recognizing that there are two pairs of fractions that sum to a whole number, as below.
(5.73 + 5.27) + (5.49 + 5.51) + 5.80 → 11 + 11 + 5.80 → 27.80

Scoring Information

Give a total score out of 3.
Give a score of 1 for the correct answer.
Give a score out of 2 for the working.

Q28.
Part A
The number 3.8 should be plotted on the number line.

Part B
Answer
4

Explanation
The student should explain how you can tell that the number is closer to 4 than 3.

Scoring Information
Give a total score out of 3.
Give a score of 1 for the number correctly plotted in Part A.
Give a score of 1 for the correct answer in Part B.
Give a score out of 1 for the explanation.

Q29.
Part A
6000 mm and 6 m should be circled.

Part B
Answer
0.006 kilometers

Work
The answer should show an understanding that 1 m = 100 cm and 1 km = 1000 m. The student may convert 600 centimeters to 6 meters and then convert 6 meters to 0.006 kilometers. The student could find that there are 100,000 cm in 1 km by multiplying 100 and 1000, and then calculate 600 ÷ 100,000 to convert 600 centimeters to kilometers.

Scoring Information
Give a total score out of 4.
Give a score of 0.5 for each number correctly circled in Part A.
Give a score of 1 for the correct answer in Part B.
Give a score out of 2 for the working in Part B.

Q30.
Part A
Answer
16 cubic centimeters

Work
The student should write and solve the equation $2 \times 2 \times 4 = 16$.

Part B
The student should identify that the volume would double if the height doubled. The student could explain that doubling one of the values in the calculation doubles the result. The student could also double the height and show that $4 \times 2 \times 4 = 32$, which is double 16.

Scoring Information
Give a total score out of 6.
Give a score of 1 for the correct answer in Part A.
Give a score out of 2 for the working in Part A.
Give a score of 1 for identifying that the volume would double in Part B.
Give a score out of 2 for the explanation in Part B.

PARCC End-Of-Year Assessment, Practice Test 2, Session 1

Question	Answer	Topic	Common Core Skill
1	0.37	Number & Operations in Base Ten	Add, subtract, multiply, and divide decimals to hundredths, using concrete models or drawings.
2	D	Number & Operations- Fractions	Interpret division of a whole number by a unit fraction, and compute such quotients.
3	A	Number & Operations- Fractions	Add and subtract fractions with unlike denominators (including mixed numbers).
4	Rhombus Kite Rectangle	Geometry	Classify two-dimensional figures in a hierarchy based on properties.
5	B	Number & Operations in Base Ten	Fluently multiply multi-digit whole numbers using the standard algorithm.
6	C	Number & Operations- Fractions	Interpret division of a unit fraction by a non-zero whole number, and compute such quotients.
7	53	Operations/Algebraic Thinking	Use parentheses, brackets, or braces in numerical expressions, and evaluate expressions with these symbols.
8	12 gallons 48 quarts 96 pints	Measurement & Data	Convert among different-sized standard measurement units within a given measurement system, and use these conversions in solving multi-step, real world problems.
9	C	Number & Operations- Fractions	Interpret a fraction as division of the numerator by the denominator.
10	D	Number & Operations- Fractions	Solve word problems involving addition and subtraction of fractions referring to the same whole, including cases of unlike denominators, e.g., by using visual fraction models or equations to represent the problem.
11	864	Number & Operations in Base Ten	Fluently multiply multi-digit whole numbers using the standard algorithm.
12	9/15 = 3/5	Number & Operations- Fractions	Interpret a fraction as division of the numerator by the denominator.
13	B	Measurement & Data	Convert among different-sized standard measurement units within a given measurement system, and use these conversions in solving multi-step, real world problems.
14	C	Operations/Algebraic Thinking	Analyze patterns and relationships by identifying apparent relationships between corresponding terms.
15	D	Number & Operations in Base Ten	Find whole-number quotients of whole numbers with up to four-digit dividends and two-digit divisors, using strategies based on properties of operations.
16	Polygon Quadrilateral Trapezoid	Geometry	Classify two-dimensional figures in a hierarchy based on properties.
17	Point Q (3, 6) Point R (6, 6) Point S (3, 3) Point T (6, 3)	Geometry	Locate a point in a coordinate system by using an ordered pair of numbers, called its coordinates.

18	$S = 0.75p$ OR $S = \frac{3}{4}p$	Operations/Algebraic Thinking	Analyze patterns and relationships by identifying apparent relationships between corresponding terms.
19	C	Measurement & Data	Recognize volume as an attribute of solid figures and understand concepts of volume measurement.
20	triangle kite pentagon	Geometry	Classify two-dimensional figures in a hierarchy based on properties.
21	B	Operations/Algebraic Thinking	Write simple expressions that record calculations with numbers, and interpret numerical expressions without evaluating them.
22	8 units	Geometry	Use a coordinate system and understand that the first number indicates how far to travel from the origin in the direction of one axis, and the second number indicates how far to travel in the direction of the second axis.
23	B	Number & Operations in Base Ten	Explain patterns in the placement of the decimal point when a decimal is multiplied or divided by a power of 10.
24	D	Number & Operations in Base Ten	Read and write decimals to thousandths using base-ten numerals, number names, and expanded form.
25	48	Operations/Algebraic Thinking	Use parentheses, brackets, or braces in numerical expressions, and evaluate expressions with these symbols.

PARCC End-Of-Year Assessment, Practice Test 2, Session 2

Question	Answer	Topic	Common Core Skill
26	A	Geometry	Classify two-dimensional figures in a hierarchy based on properties.
27	$L = 8B$	Operations/Algebraic Thinking	Analyze patterns and relationships by identifying apparent relationships between corresponding terms.
28	D	Operations/Algebraic Thinking	Write simple expressions that record calculations with numbers, and interpret numerical expressions without evaluating them.
29	55 55.1 55.15	Number & Operations in Base Ten	Use place value understanding to round decimals to any place.
30	34	Operations/Algebraic Thinking	Use parentheses, brackets, or braces in numerical expressions, and evaluate expressions with these symbols.
31	B	Operations/Algebraic Thinking	Analyze patterns and relationships by identifying apparent relationships between corresponding terms.
32	48 54 66 78	Number & Operations in Base Ten	Find whole-number quotients of whole numbers with up to four-digit dividends and two-digit divisors, using strategies based on place value, the properties of operations, and/or the relationship between multiplication and division.
33	July May June April	Number & Operations in Base Ten	Compare two decimals to thousandths based on meanings of the digits in each place, using >, =, and < symbols to record the results of comparisons.
34	Small	Number & Operations-Fractions	Interpret a fraction as division of the numerator by the denominator. Solve word problems involving division of whole numbers leading to answers in the form of fractions or mixed numbers.
35	C	Operations/Algebraic Thinking	Analyze patterns and relationships by identifying apparent relationships between corresponding terms.
36	4.18 < 4.50 < 4.59 < 4.61 < 4.73	Number & Operations in Base Ten	Compare two decimals to thousandths based on meanings of the digits in each place, using >, =, and < symbols to record the results of comparisons.
37	6	Number & Operations in Base Ten	Find whole-number quotients of whole numbers with up to four-digit dividends and two-digit divisors, using strategies based on the relationship between multiplication and division.
38	1st, 2nd, and 6th	Number & Operations in Base Ten	Illustrate and explain calculations by using equations, rectangular arrays, and/or area models.
39	D	Number & Operations in Base Ten	Explain patterns in the placement of the decimal point when a decimal is multiplied or divided by a power of 10.
40	D	Geometry	Understand that attributes belonging to a category of two-dimensional figures also belong to all subcategories of that category.

41	A	Number & Operations-Fractions	Explaining why multiplying a given number by a fraction greater than 1 results in a product greater than the given number.
42	C	Operations/Algebraic Thinking	Generate two numerical patterns using two given rules. Identify apparent relationships between corresponding terms.
43	D	Number & Operations in Base Ten	Perform operations with multi-digit whole numbers.
44	2nd and 5th	Number & Operations in Base Ten	Perform operations with multi-digit whole numbers.
45	D	Number & Operations in Base Ten	Find whole-number quotients of whole numbers. Illustrate and explain the calculation by using equations, rectangular arrays, and/or area models.
46	D	Operations/Algebraic Thinking	Write simple expressions that record calculations with numbers, and interpret numerical expressions without evaluating them.
47	B	Operations/Algebraic Thinking	Analyze patterns and relationships by identifying apparent relationships between corresponding terms.
48	A	Geometry	Classify two-dimensional figures in a hierarchy based on properties.
49	600 60 6	Number & Operations in Base Ten	Recognize that in a multi-digit number, a digit in one place represents 10 times as much as it represents in the place to its right and 1/10 of what it represents in the place to its left.
50	C	Number & Operations-Fractions	Interpret multiplication as scaling (resizing) by comparing the size of a product to the size of one factor on the basis of the size of the other factor, without performing the indicated multiplication.

Made in the USA
Lexington, KY
29 March 2015